I Can Tell the Truth

Doing the Right Thing

Written by Jenette Donovan Guntly

Illustrated by Keiko Motoyama

Please visit our web site at: www.garethstevens.com
For a free color catalog describing Gareth Stevens Publishing's list of high-quality books
and multimedia programs, call 1-800-542-2595 (USA) or 1-800-387-3178 (Canada).
Gareth Stevens Publishing's fax: (414) 332-3567.

Library of Congress Cataloging-in-Publication Data

Guntly, Jenette Donovan.
    (Telling the truth)
    I can tell the truth / written by Jenette Donovan Guntly; illustrated by Keiko Motoyama.
        p. cm. — (Doing the right thing)
    ISBN 0-8368-4249-9 (lib. bdg.)
    1. Honesty—Juvenile literature. I. Motoyama, Keiko. II. Title.
    BJ1533.H7G86   2004
    179'.9—dc22   2004045312

This North American edition first published in 2005 by
Gareth Stevens Publishing
A World Almanac Education Group Company
330 West Olive Street, Suite 100
Milwaukee, WI 53212 USA

This edition copyright © 2005 by Gareth Stevens, Inc. Original edition copyright © 2002 by Creative Teaching Press, Inc.,
P.O. Box 2723, Huntington Beach, CA 92647-0723. First published in the United States in 2002 as *Telling the Truth:
Learning about Honesty, Integrity, and Trustworthiness* by Creative Teaching Press, Inc. Original text copyright © 2002
by Regina G. Burch.

Illustrator: Keiko Motoyama
Gareth Stevens designer: Kami M. Koenig

Printed in the United States of America

1 2 3 4 5 6 7 8 9 08 07 06 05 04

I can tell the truth!

I want to be class president.

I say, "Please vote for me."

Steve asks for something I can't do.

I answer honestly.

When Tammy wants to see my test,

I say, "Cheating's wrong."

I always tell my friends the truth.

It makes our friendships strong.

We all should try to do our best

in everything we do.

I'm proud that my friends count on me

Our Class President

to always follow through.

"Always tell the truth," I say.
"The truth earns trust in every way."